Making Difficult Words Easy

Code Reader Books provide codes with "sound keys" to help read difficult words. For example, a word that may be difficult to read is "unicorn," so it might be followed by a code like this: unicorn *(YOO-nih-korn)*. By providing codes with phonetic sound keys, Code Reader Books make reading easier and more enjoyable.

Examples of Code Reader™ Keys

Long a sound (as in make):
a *(with a silent e)* or **ay**
Examples: able *(AY-bul)*; break *(brake)*

Short i sound (as in sit): **i** or **ih**
Examples: myth *(mith)*; mission *(MIH-shun)*

Long i sound (as in by):
i *(with a silent e)* or **y**
Examples: might *(mite)*; bicycle *(BY-sih-kul)*

Keys for the long o sound (as in hope):
o *(with a silent e)* or **oh**
Examples: molten *(MOLE-ten)*; ocean *(OH-shen)*

Codes use dashes between syllables *(SIH-luh-buls)*, and stressed syllables have capital letters.

To see more Code Reader sound keys, see page 44.

How Animals Talk

How Animals Talk

A Code Reader™ Chapter Book
Blue Series

This book was created by Reimagined Classroom
under agreement with Treasure Bay, Inc.

With special thanks to Emma Kocina, biologist at the California Academy
of Sciences, for her review of the information in this book

Text Copyright © 2025 Treasure Bay, Inc.
All rights reserved

Photos provided by iStock

Reading Consultant: Jennifer L. VanSlander, Ph.D., Asst. Professor of
Educational Leadership, Columbus State University

Code Reader™ is a trademark of Treasure Bay, Inc.

Patent Pending. Code Reader books are designed using an innovative
system of methods to create and include phonetic codes to enhance the
readability of text. Reserved rights include any patent rights.

Published by
Treasure Bay, Inc.
PO Box 519
Roseville, CA 95661 USA

Printed in China

Library of Congress Control Number: 2024944961

ISBN: 978-1-60115-724-9

Visit us online at:
CodeReader.org

PR-1-25

CONTENTS

Chapter 1: Do Animals Talk? *(tawk)* 2

Chapter 2: Talking with Sounds 4

Chapter 3: Talking with Signals *(SIG-nulz)* 14

Chapter 4: Talking with Touch *(tuch)* 24

Chapter 5: Talking with Smell 32

Chapter 6: Talking with Humans *(HYOO-menz)* 39

Glossary 42

Questions to Think About 43

Sound Keys for Codes 44

1 | Do Animals Talk? *(TAWK)*

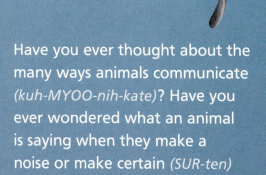

Have you ever thought about the many ways animals communicate *(kuh-MYOO-nih-kate)*? Have you ever wondered what an animal is saying when they make a noise or make certain *(SUR-ten)* movements?

Animals may not be able to talk using *(YOO-zing)* words, but animals have lots of ways to communicate or "talk" with each other.

In this book, you will learn *(lurn)* about some of the ways animals speak to each other.

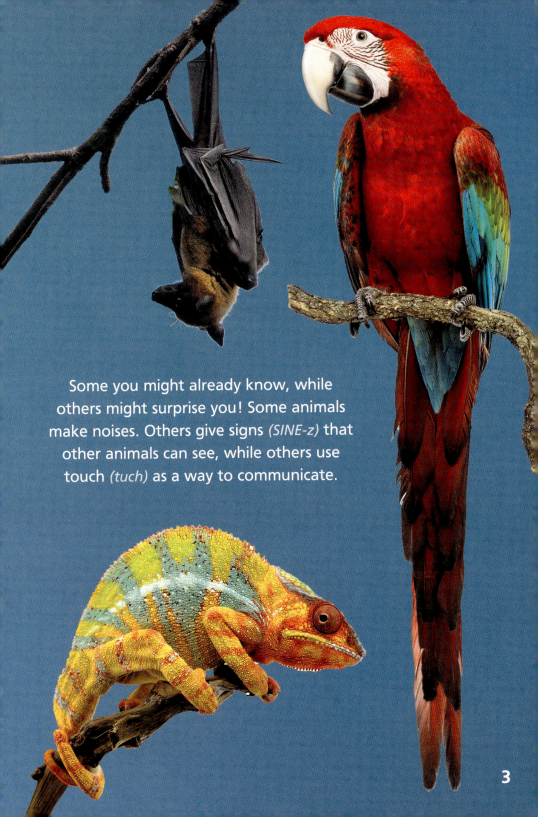

Some you might already know, while others might surprise you! Some animals make noises. Others give signs *(SINE-z)* that other animals can see, while others use touch *(tuch)* as a way to communicate.

2 TALKING WITH SOUNDS

Animals use sounds like howls, barks, or chirps to communicate, or speak, with each other.

CHIRP CHIRP

CHIRP CHIRP

RIBBIT

Some sounds are very loud and are heard over long distances *(DIS-stan-sez)*. Others are quiet and only heard by animals that are close by.

WOOF

Some sounds act as warnings to other animals in a group that a predator *(PREH-duh-tur)* is close by. Others are used to attract mates, give a warning to other animals to stay away, or defend their territory *(TARE-ih-tor-ree)*.

WOLVES

One way that wolves *(wulvz)* communicate is through *(throo)* sounds. Howling is one example of how wolves communicate with each other.

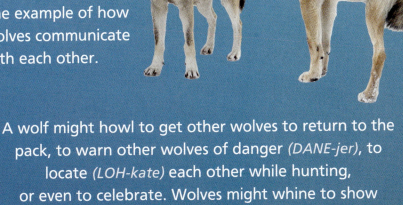

A wolf might howl to get other wolves to return to the pack, to warn other wolves of danger *(DANE-jer)*, to locate *(LOH-kate)* each other while hunting, or even to celebrate. Wolves might whine to show they are anxious *(ANG-chus)* or whimper to show they want to be friendly.

If a wolf growls, it is a warning. The wolf wants to be seen as a threat *(thret)*. The wolf may be saying it will attack to defend itself, other wolves, or its territory.

BIRDS

Most birds communicate using sounds called call notes.

Birds use different call notes to speak with each other. Just like you might use a different tone of voice *(voys)* to show others you are excited or scared, birds use different call notes.

Call notes also sound different depending on the type *(tipe)* of bird. A sparrow's call notes sound like chirping, but a larger bird's call notes sound like squawks *(skwawks)*.

A baby bird will chirp for its mother to return to the nest with food. A mockingbird might squawk at a bird that is too close to its nest.

Birds communicate to warn about danger, to signal to certain members of their flock or group *(groop)*, or to let other birds know where to find food and water.

Birds pass down their sounds to their babies by singing or using call notes. The baby birds learn how to communicate with other birds by repeating those sounds.

BATS

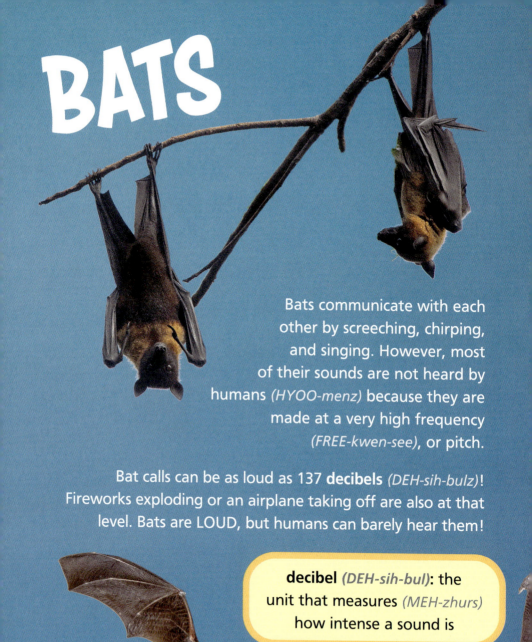

Bats communicate with each other by screeching, chirping, and singing. However, most of their sounds are not heard by humans *(HYOO-menz)* because they are made at a very high frequency *(FREE-kwen-see)*, or pitch.

Bat calls can be as loud as 137 **decibels** *(DEH-sih-bulz)*! Fireworks exploding or an airplane taking off are also at that level. Bats are LOUD, but humans can barely hear them!

decibel *(DEH-sih-bul)*: the unit that measures *(MEH-zhurs)* how intense a sound is

Each bat has a unique *(yoo-NEEK)*, or special, voice used to call others.

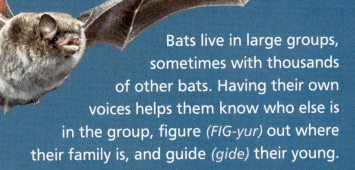

Bats live in large groups, sometimes with thousands of other bats. Having their own voices helps them know who else is in the group, figure *(FIG-yur)* out where their family is, and guide *(gide)* their young.

Bats use **echolocation** *(eh-coh-loh-KAY-shun)*. This helps them to find their way in the dark and find flying insects to eat.

echolocation *(eh-koh-loh-KAY-shun)*: using the echoes from sound waves bouncing off of objects to find where something is

Since most bats are **nocturnal** *(nok-TUR-nul)*, echolocation helps them know what is out there in the darkness.

nocturnal *(nok-TUR-nul)*: active or awake at night

9

WHALES

Whales are talkative *(TAWK-uh-tiv)* animals. In their pods, or groups, they use different noises—like clicks, squeaks, whistles *(WIH-suls)*, and songs—to communicate with each other.

The male humpback whale can sing a song that is 30 minutes *(MIN-its)* long and repeat it for hours. They sing to attract mates, while eating, and when moving to other areas.

Similar to how bats use echolocation, whales use clicks to locate objects.

Different pods of whales have their own dialects *(DY-uh-lekts)*, or ways of speaking.

DOLPHINS

Like whales, dolphins use whistles and clicks to communicate.

Dolphins also use clicks to locate objects. Dolphin clicks are made at higher frequencies *(FREE-kwen-seez)* that do not travel as far, so they cannot locate objects at long distances.

Scientists *(SY-en-tists)* think that every bottlenose dolphin has a unique whistle called a signature *(SIG-nuh-chur)* whistle. Much like humans use names, this whistle can be used by dolphins to identify *(I-DEN-tih-fy)* each other when communicating.

Dolphins also use sounds called burst pulses. These are very loud and quick sounds that dolphins use to chase sharks away and to ensure *(en-SHUR)* their young are safe.

11

FROGS

Each frog species *(SPEE-sheez)* makes a unique call, or sound, much like humans have different accents *(AK-sents)*.

Large frogs have deeper calls, while smaller frogs have higher calls. The weather *(WEH-thur)* can also affect a frog's call. Warmer weather lets frogs vocalize *(VOH-kuh-lize)*, or use their calls, faster.

The most common way male frogs communicate is by singing songs to attract female *(FEE-male)* frogs. Males will find a nice spot near water to sing their songs. This is because frogs lay their eggs in water.

Several frogs may call at once *(wuns)* to attract females. However, male frogs can add a warning call to their song to warn other males to keep their distance. This is also a way to defend their territory.

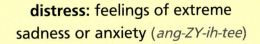

distress: feelings of extreme sadness or anxiety *(ang-ZY-ih-tee)*

Male and female frogs can make **distress** calls. If a frog is attacked, they will scream. Sometimes the scream is loud enough *(ee-NUF)* to scare the predator, and the frog can escape.

3 TALKING WITH SIGNALS

Visual *(VIH-zhoo-ul)* communication means using signals that can be seen. These signals could include facial *(FAY-shul)* expressions, movements, **postures** *(POS-churz)*, and colors.

> **posture** *(POS-chur)*: how an animal or person positions *(puh-ZIH-shuns)* their body when standing or sitting

Animals may use these signals to warn other animals, attract mates, blend in with their surroundings to protect themselves from predators, or even to show that they are poisonous *(POY-zuh-nuhs)*.

These visual signs can let other animals and humans know how the animal is feeling or how to behave. For example, a female rabbit will use her white tail as a visual signal for her babies to follow while going back to their home.

CHAMELEONS

Chameleons *(kuh-MEE-lee-uns)* can quickly change the color of their body, and they can communicate using these color changes. Each time a chameleon changes its color, it is sending an important message *(MEH-sij)* to other chameleons.

Male chameleons' coloring becomes brighter when they are protecting their territory or attracting females. They can change their color from red to white to green in seconds. When male chameleons fight, the chameleon whose *(hooz)* head changes color faster is most likely to win the fight.

Chameleons can also change their color to blend in with their environment *(en-VY-urn-ment)* or adjust their body temperature *(TEM-pruh-chur)*.

15

PEACOCKS

Male and female peacocks look very different. Female peacocks are called peahens. They have brown feathers *(FEH-thurz)*.

Male peacocks have large, brightly colored tails that spread *(spred)* out around them. A peacock's tail can have over 200 feathers that are green, blue, red, or gold with spots that look like eyes.

One way that male peacocks communicate with females is by fanning out their large tail feathers. They also shake and rattle their feathers to make them shimmer, or shine.

16

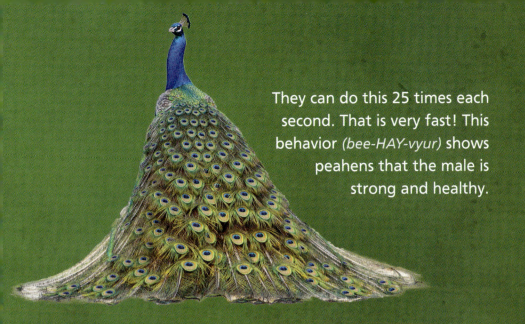

They can do this 25 times each second. That is very fast! This behavior *(bee-HAY-vyur)* shows peahens that the male is strong and healthy.

Peacocks also fan out their tail feathers to warn other male peacocks to stay away from their area *(AIR-ree-uh)* or certain females.

If a peacock is threatened *(THREH-tind)*, it will fan out its tail feathers to appear larger and to scare predators.

FIREFLIES

Fireflies *(FIRE-flyz)* have a very small organ *(OR-gen)* called a lantern on the underside of their stomachs *(STUH-meks)* that lights up. Fireflies use this light to communicate with each other in the dark.

LANTERN

Different types of fireflies use different patterns of flashes to recognize *(REH-cug-nize)* each other, to attract mates, and even to trick predators. They also flash in different colors, like yellow, green, and orange.

North American *(uh-MAIR-ih-ken)* male fireflies fly through the air at night and signal to female fireflies. When a female firefly sees a signal she likes, she flashes her light back. Then the male firefly flies to meet her.

Some fireflies flash their lights for hours. Others flash for a few minutes or at certain times, like when the sun is setting.

Fireflies might flash their lights at sunset to escape predators. Their yellow or green flashes blend in more easily with the trees and grass because there is still sunlight.

PENGUINS

Penguins *(PEN-gwinz)* are some of the most social *(SOH-shul)* animals. They live in large groups and have certain ways of communicating how they are feeling.

One way that penguins communicate is through movements of their head, neck, or wings. These movements can be different depending on the type of penguin.

Many species, or types, of penguins wave their beaks or flap their flippers. Others puff up their chests or spread their wings. There are different reasons *(REE-zunz)* for each behavior, such as defending territory, attracting a mate, or showing **dominance** *(DAH-mih-nens)*.

dominance *(DAH-mih-nens)*: being in control or in charge

When a penguin reaches its flippers out and lifts its beak, it may be showing that it is friendly and wants to avoid fighting with other penguins as it moves through a group.

Some penguins move their necks in a special way as a way to say "hello" to each other.

When penguins are looking for mates, they might bow to each other to show that they are friendly and to make each other more comfortable *(KUM-fur-tuh-bul)*.

COBRAS

Cobras *(COH-bruz)* are not social animals. One way they communicate is through visual cues.

Cobras like to have their own territory. They do not like it when other snakes or predators enter it.

hood: skin on a cobra's neck that expands

Cobras have **hoods** around their heads. If a cobra is threatened, it will spread its hood and rise up to intimidate *(in-TIH-mih-date)*, or scare, the other animal. A cobra can lift up to one-third of the length of its body. A king cobra can grow up to 18 feet long!

This behavior gives the other animal a warning to leave the cobra alone or to move out of its territory. This behavior might be enough to scare a predator and give the cobra time to escape.

Another way that cobras communicate is through wrestling *(REH-sling)*. Male cobras will wrestle *(REH-sul)* each other to impress other male cobras and show their dominance. The first one to get the other's head on the ground wins.

4 Talking with Touch

Tactile *(TAK-tile)* communication is the most common type of animal communication. This type of communication involves touching *(TUH-ching)*. Animals must be close together to communicate in this way. This lets them share messages *(MEH-suh-jez)* with each other quickly.

Touch helps large groups of animals get to know each other better and keep things peaceful. Animals are able *(AY-bul)* to form strong bonds, or friendships, with each other through this type of communication.

Tactile communication can include caring for babies, grooming each other, or socializing *(SOH-shuh-ly-zing)*.

Dogs

One way that dogs communicate is through tactile communication. Dogs use touch to **impress** other dogs or to bond with other dogs.

A dog might try to **impress** another dog by putting its paws on the other dog's back or its mouth on the other dog's neck. These actions show that one dog is in charge.

impress: to make someone like you or think of you in a good way

Dogs often lick each other to say hello or wrestle with each other to play.

Dogs also communicate with humans using tactile communication. They can "shake hands," sit in a person's lap, or lick their owners.

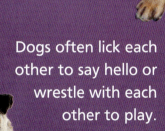

HORSES

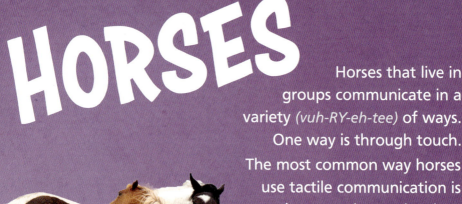

Horses that live in groups communicate in a variety *(vuh-RY-eh-tee)* of ways. One way is through touch. The most common way horses use tactile communication is by grooming each other. This helps horses form strong relationships *(ree-LAY-shun-ships)* with each other. When horses **groom** each other, it helps them remain calm *(kom)* and provides comfort.

Horses will greet each other by touching their noses *(NOH-zez)* together. If a horse is friendly with another horse, it might also gently hit the other horse with its muzzle *(MUH-zul)* or lay its head on that horse's rump.

grooming: cleaning the coat, or hair, of an animal

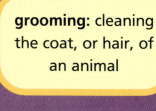

MUZZLE

Some groups of horses like to play with each other. This is another way horses communicate through touch. They might bump into each other or nip at and chase each other as they try to get the other horse's attention.

Not every touch is nice, though. If horses are angry *(ANG-gree)* at each other, they can bite or run into each other with a lot of force. These behaviors are done to show dominance or to warn another horse to stay away.

MONKEYS

Tactile communication is very important for all types of monkeys. Touch is important to comfort each other, attract mates, and establish which monkeys are in charge within the group.

All monkeys groom each other. They help each other clean their skin and fur. Grooming also makes friendships stronger, helps them **apologize** *(uh-PAH-luh-jize)* to each other, and helps to keep the peace in large groups. This is important because monkeys can live in groups of several hundred monkeys in one place.

> **apologize** *(uh-PAH-luh-jize)*: to say that you are sorry for something

Smaller monkeys groom larger or more dominant monkeys, and in return they get protection and acceptance *(ak-SEP-tens)* within the group.

Female monkeys hold and even cuddle their babies. This allows the baby monkeys to feel safe and protected with their mothers.

Like other animals, monkeys like to play with each other. They may playfully hit or grab each other. This behavior could also be to alert other monkeys to danger or to sources *(SOR-sez)* of food.

LIONS

Lions *(LY-unz)* are the most social group of wild cats. They live in groups called *prides*. Lions communicate in different ways, and one way is through touch.

Lions perform a greeting ceremony *(SEH-ruh-moh-nee)* to welcome back lions that have been away from the pride. They sniff each other's noses, rub heads, and rub against *(uh-GENST)* each other. Lion cubs, or baby lions, also join in and rub against their parents' chests or throats.

Lions also groom each other, usually *(YOO-zhoo-uh-lee)* by licking the other lion's fur.

ELEPHANTS

Elephants are very **tactile** animals. They use many parts of their bodies, like their trunks, ears, feet, and tails, to touch each other.

tactile: describing *(des-KRY-bing)* the sense of touch

Elephants use their trunks to reassure *(ree-uh-SHUR)* each other, to guide *(gide)* a baby elephant, or to touch and push each other when playing. They also reach their trunks out and wrap them around another elephant's trunk for comfort or **reassurance** *(ree-uh-SHUR-uns)*.

reassurance *(ree-uh-SHUR-uns)*: using words or touch to make someone or something feel better

5 TALKING WITH SMELL

Animal bodies can produce *(proh-DOOS)* certain smells that can send messages to other animals. These smells are called **pheromones** *(FARE-uh-mohnz)*.

> **pheromones** *(FARE-uh-mohnz)*: special chemical *(KEM-ih-kul)* scents, or smells, that an animal produces *(proh-DOO-sez)* in its body that sends messages to other animals

Each smell has a certain message. These scents can travel through the air, or be spread on the ground or other surfaces *(SUR-fuh-sez)*. Animals use their senses of taste and smell to "read" these messages. The messages could be about territory, mating, food, or danger. Pheromones are made in certain **glands** of an animal's body. The pheromones can be sent out in different ways depending on the type of animal.

> **glands**: small organs found all over the body that make something the body needs

32

ANTS

Ants communicate with other members of their colony *(KAH-luh-nee)*, or group, using pheromones. It is important that ants can communicate quickly because they live with thousands of other ants in one colony.

They use their **antennae** *(an-TEH-nee)* to "smell" these chemicals and communicate things like what is happening in the colony and where other ants can find food.

> **antennae** *(an-TEN-nee)*: a pair of long body parts on an insect's head. (If there is just one, the word is antenna *(an-TEN-nuh)*.)

They use pheromones to quickly send messages to other ants to alert them to danger, such as when a predator is coming or that part of the nest has been destroyed.

BEES

Bees use pheromones to interact with other bees and to manage *(MAN-ij)* their very large colonies *(KAH-luh-neez)*. Like ants, bees smell these chemicals using their antennae.

There are different groups of bees within each colony, and they release different types of pheromones for different jobs.

One type is the alarm pheromone. This is used to tell other bees to defend their colony from intruders *(in-TROO-durz)*, including predators like bears or skunks.

Another type is called the Nasonov *(nah-SOH-nof)* pheromone. Bees use this to guide bees back to the hive, bring more worker bees to a swarm, and to lead other bees to food and water sources.

Worker bees also release a special pheromone to stop baby bees from maturing *(muh-CHUR-ing)*, or growing up, so quickly. This is to keep the number of young and adult bees in the colony balanced *(BAL-inst)*, or even.

CATS

Cats communicate using pheromones from glands in their bodies found on their chins, ears, cheeks, tails, backs, and paw pads. The messages they send can only be noticed *(NOH-tist)* by other cats.

One way cats use pheromones to communicate is by rubbing or bumping against things. This is called *marking*.

When a cat rubs against something, it releases pheromones from its head that let other cats know that this is its territory. A cat can also use these pheromones to show other cats that an object is safe for them.

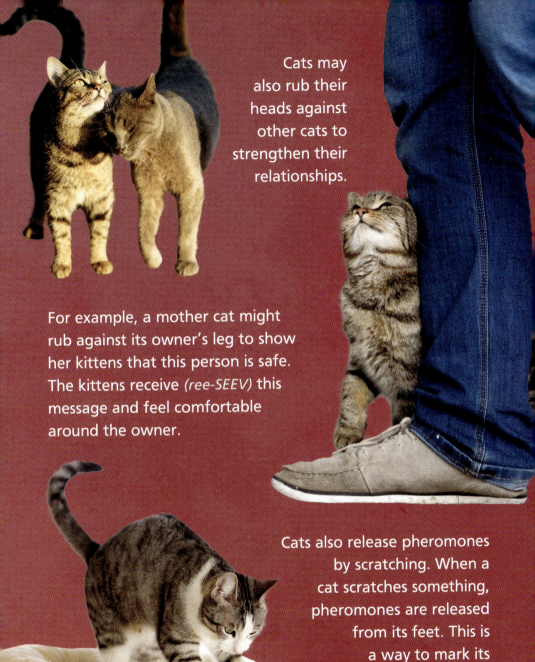

Cats may also rub their heads against other cats to strengthen their relationships.

For example, a mother cat might rub against its owner's leg to show her kittens that this person is safe. The kittens receive *(ree-SEEV)* this message and feel comfortable around the owner.

Cats also release pheromones by scratching. When a cat scratches something, pheromones are released from its feet. This is a way to mark its territory and make it feel safe in its home.

MICE

Mice are able to communicate using pheromones in their **urine** *(YUR-in)*. Both male and female mice are able to communicate different messages in this way.

urine *(YUR-in)*: liquid *(LIH-kwid)* waste, or pee, that the kidneys *(KID-neez)* produce and that is released from the body

Each male mouse has a **specific** *(speh-SIH-fik)* pheromone in its urine that marks his territory. When mice travel away from their homes, they use these scents to identify other mice's territory and know to stay away.

These pheromones also alert mice to which ones are more dominant, or powerful, than others.

6 TALKING WITH HUMANS

Humans can communicate with animals through visual, auditory *(AW-dih-tor-ree)*, and tactile communication.

Whether it is a dog barking at its owner to ask for a treat, a monkey holding a zookeeper's hand for comfort, or a cat rubbing against its owner's legs, humans and animals can send messages back and forth.

Many scientists have worked to understand how animals communicate and have tried to imitate, or copy, those behaviors and sounds to see if animals could understand those same communication signals from a human.

CHIMPANZEES

Chimpanzees use many different sounds, gestures *(JES-churz)*, and facial expressions to communicate. The way they communicate with each other shows that they are able to understand each other on a deeper level than other animals.

Chimpanzees can use hand gestures to communicate. Scientists have been able to teach them sign language *(SINE LANG-gwej)* to communicate with humans and with other chimpanzees. Chimpanzees that learn sign language have shown they are able to invent new signs and combine signs to say different words.

PARROTS

Parrots can speak to humans using actual *(AK-shoo-ul)* language! Parrots learn human languages in phases *(FAY-zez)*, or parts. Phase *(faze)* one starts at birth. The baby parrot "babbles," or makes noises that do not mean anything.

Phase two happens when a parrot can make connections between words they have heard before and new words. The parrot will repeat what its humans say.

Phase three starts when the parrot understands how sounds they hear are connected to ideas. They understand that words have meaning and learn how to use them to communicate. For example, parrots can ask for certain treats to eat or to be picked up by their owners.

GLOSSARY

cue *(kyoo)***:** something said or done that gives a signal to a person or animal

expression *(ex-SPREH-shun)***:** a look on the face that shows how a person or animal is feeling

gesture *(JES-chur)***:** a movement made by a part of the body that represents, or shows, an idea or feeling

predator *(PREH-duh-tur)***:** an animal that eats other animals

social *(SOH-shul):* enjoying being with others

species *(SPEE-sheez)***:** a group of animals with the same characteristics or traits

territory *(TARE-uh-tor-ree)***:** an area that an animal has chosen to defend so that it can hunt, mate, or nest there

whistle *(WIH-sul)***:** a loud, high-pitched sound

QUESTIONS TO THINK ABOUT

1. Which way of communicating do you think is the easiest to understand? Which is the most difficult? Why?

2. What is an interesting fact you learned about the way animals communicate?

3. If you were able to talk to one of these animals, which one would it be? Why?

4. Imagine that you could talk to animals. What questions would you ask them?

5. Do you think it would good or bad if people could talk with animals? What might be good about it? Why might it be bad?

Making Difficult Words Easy

Code Reader Books provide codes with "sound keys" to help read difficult words. For example, a word that may be challenging to read is "chameleon," so it might be followed by a code like this: chameleon *(kuh-MEE-lee-un)*.

The codes use phonetic keys for each sound in the word. Knowing the keys can help make reading the codes easier.

Code Reader™ Keys

Long a sound (as in make):
a *(with a silent e)*, **ai**, or **ay**
Examples: break *(brake)*;
area *(AIR-ee-uh)*; able *(AY-bul)*

Short a sound (as in cat): **a**
Example: practice *(PRAK-tis)*

Long e sound (as in keep): **ee**
Example: complete *(kum-PLEET)*

Short e sound (as in set): **e** or **eh**
Examples: metric *(MEH-trik)*;
bread *(bred)*

Long i sound (as in by):
i *(with a silent e)* or **y**
Examples: might *(mite)*;
bicycle *(BY-sih-kul)*

Short i sound (as in sit): **i** or **ih**
Examples: myth *(mith)*;
condition *(kun-DIH-shun)*

Long u sound (as in cube): **yoo**
Example: unicorn *(YOO-nih-korn)*

Short u or schwa sound (as in cup):
u or **uh**
Examples: pension *(PEN-shun)*;
about *(uh-BOWT)*

Long o sound (as in hope):
o *(with a silent e)*, **oh**,
or **o** at the end of a syllable
Examples: molten *(MOLE-ten)*;
ocean *(OH-shen)*; nobody *(NO-bah-dee)*

Short o sound (as in top): **o** or **ah**
Examples: posture *(POS-chur)*;
bother *(BAH-ther)*

Long oo sound (as in cool): **oo**
Example: school *(skool)*

Short oo sound (as in look): **o͝o**
Examples: wood *(wo͝od)*;
could *(ko͝od)*

oy sound (as in boy): **oy**
Example: boisterous *(BOY-stur-us)*

ow sound (as in cow): **ow**
Example: discount *(DIS-kownt)*

aw sound (as in paw): **aw**
Example: faucet *(FAW-sit)*

qu sound (as in quit): **kw**
Example: question *(KWES-chun)*

zh sound (as in garage): **zh**
Example: fission *(FIH-zhun)*